LEARN TO READ TAROT AND CRYSTAL BALL

BY

MARK HOWARD

TABLE OF CONTENTS

INTRODUCTION

Many people struggle or have issues with reading tarot and much of this is due to a simple fact that they have been taught incorrectly in how to read and what tarot actually is used for.

The majority of books and those that teach tarot will tell you that you need to learn the specific meaning of every card in the deck, and although this may sound like the logical way to learning tarot, it is, in fact, the wrong way.

Tarot is not a memory game! Although we place the cards in certain spreads and positions to determine what the card is representing to that person at that time (i.e. a past card), it does not mean that each card has the same meaning for every person.

Take into consideration the Two of Swords, where its literal meaning refers to a division or parting of ways, may have a bearing for one person but not everyone.

As you start to develop and do your own readings, you may find that certain cards will have a specific meaning for you. One of the examples of this is a reader who found that the Two of Swords actually indicated that the person would have an issue or accident with their car and that every person she read for that got that card indeed had problems.

To read tarot is therefore not necessarily knowing all the literal meanings of every card. The most important aspect is to know and understand the general overview of the four minor arcana (lesser secrets) suits and possibly to understand four of the major arcana (great secrets) cards which are often miss-understood.

One of my students (who has learned to read tarot from this book) told me about how she and a friend got together to do a reading for each other. This is, of course, a brilliant idea and one that I fully encourage all my students to do along with reading for themselves.

On the day of the reading, her friend (who was taught by learning all the card meanings), gave a reading and had to refer to the training manual for the card meanings (it is also worth noting that the course she did took over 8 weeks to complete). The reading in all aspects was an Ok reading and although much of it had no bearing for my student, it was a passable reading to give.

My student then gave her reading and this, of course, relied on no student notes, and the information she gave was amazing. She provided timeframes, information that was relevant to her friend and even clarified information that her friend had been looking for.

At the end of the reading, my student's friend was amazed and asked how many years had she been doing readings, only to be shocked to hear that it was her first-ever reading and that she only took a day to learn how to read the tarot cards themselves.

This story is in no means a way for me to say how great my students are, but more to highlight that many people are given poor advice and training because that's how the trainer was trained!

Tarot is a developing art form and as you grow and develop you will find that your readings and how you read will change over time as well.

You may also be asking why read Tarot and Crystal ball as this book will teach you? The answer is that these two forms of divination complement each other extremely well. When you start reading you will find that you can give more information and direction if you include the crystal ball as part of the reading process.

If you consider tarot to be like Morse code, then crystal ball is more your video conferencing – it really is that different but with the two you have a powerful set of tools at your disposal.

Regardless if you are new to tarot or an experienced reader, learning and having new ways to read is always exciting as well as a great way to build upon your experiences. The exciting news is that the methods I show you can be used for your own readings, reading for friends and even for distance reading too. The majority of my readings to date are now distance and sent via emails…. but more about this later.

Included in this book are 14 easy to use spreads including one given to me by my guides. By using these spreads you are able to give readings that will allow you to pinpoint certain actions or potential events for your clients at that time of the reading. You will also see that I never go past a year for a reading as after a year the reading tends to become very generic and with people changing their paths, it won't necessarily be as accurate either.

It's easy to have fun with Tarot and crystal ball readings, and although you may give messages people do not always want to hear, it's always better to be forewarned of a potential event than to walk into it blind.

Again this is something I encourage students to do. As much as I would love to give positive readings all the time, it simply does not work that way.

One client once said to me, that if I had not warned her of the issues she would be facing that year, she honestly would not have made it through those six months. It was the fact that I said after this period of challenges and problems, things were going to be better and more positive for her, was she able to look forward to coming six months and get through her initial problems without too much trouble.

HISTORY OF TAROT AND CRYSTAL BALL

The ancestors of what we today know as Tarot cards can be traced back to around the late fourteenth century. Artists in Europe created the first playing cards, which were used for games, and featured four different suits. These suits were similar to what we still use today – staves or wands, discs or coins, cups, and swords. After a decade or two of using these, in the mid-1400s, Italian artists began painting additional cards, heavily illustrated, to add to the existing suits.

In both France and Italy, the original purpose of the Tarot was as a parlor game, not as a divinatory tool. It appears that divination with playing cards started to become popular in the late sixteenth and early seventeenth century, although at that time, it was far simpler than the way we use Tarot today.

By the eighteenth century, however, people were beginning to assign specific meanings to each card, and even offer suggestions as to how they could be laid out for divinatory purposes. This, of course, brings me back to the issues of having specific meanings for each card.

The fact that playing cards were used as an early form of tarot and divination always makes me laugh. As you can imagine a lot of people (notably those from a strong religious faith) will say that tarot is evil.

Now I'm not going to get into a discussion about religion and divination (that's for another book), but when people start to give me their personal and religious views on Tarot I always ask if they have any playing cards (more often than not they do). When I point out that they feel that tarot is evil but playing cards which are the original tarot is allowed into their homes, it can be fun and yes is very naughty of me to do.

The point is Tarot and Crystal ball is not evil, that again is just one segment of people's views which is fine. Then again you need to ask yourself why more than 80% of my clients are devoted Christian, Hindu, Muslim, and Jews…. again maybe that will be for another book, another day!

Unlike Tarot, the earliest use of a crystal ball can be first attributed to the Celtic Druids who divined the future and omens with beryl balls. Many reading would include the outcome of battles and conflicts or simple to get answers to questions such as how a harvest would be that year.

Interesting if you look throughout history, leaders such as Winston Churchill and President Lincoln actually had psychics to help them to prepare for battles and predict the outcome of a certain strategy.

Crystal ball really seemed to fade away during the '70s with more readers preferring using Tarot, but today more and more readers and using both forms of divination to give readings. In fact, a good friend of mine recently said that he has started to use his decks a lot less preferring using the crystal ball as a form of divination to help develop his third eye and his connection with his guides.

Saying that still, there are more tarot readers than crystal ball readers!

HOW TO CHOOSE YOUR DECK

Each tarot deck is specific to the user and the best way to purchase your deck is to meditate on it. Visit the store you are getting your deck from and once there, sit on the floor and ask your Spirit Guide(s) to direct you to the pack you should be using.

If you are not Intune with your guides then use your gut instinct. In fact, most of the work you will be doing in this book will require you to use instincts and go with these each time.

I recall my first deck and whilst sitting on the floor asked my guides which is my deck out of the book shelve filled with over 100 decks. It's also very interesting sitting on the floor doing this as you tend to find other people in the shop giving wide berth the "strange person" sitting on the floor.

As I looked up at about 8 shelves of decks, my guide asked me to go to the third shelve from the top, and take the tenth deck from the left. Doing as instructed I picked up the deck and instantly felt that the deck was wrong – it did not sit well for me and I was confused. Querying this my guide asked me to put the deck back and recount which I did, but as I went to the first deck I was told to stop. It turned out the deck I thought was the first, as in fact not and there was another deck in front of it which I had not seen. Counting again took me to my deck and straight away I could feel it was the right one for me.

Once you have your deck, purchase some Indian Silk which is the purest silk you can purchase. The cards should always be wrapped in this silk when they are not being used.

Take the cards out of the pack and ask your Spirit Guide(s) to join you in blessing the cards, before cleansing them and then wrapping them in their silk till needed.

It is also worth getting a tarot cloth or use a cloth to do your readings on. This allows you to have the cards on a surface which you know is clean and easy to use.

Many people ask about cards given as gifts and what they should do with these. The simple approach is to hold them in your hand and close your eyes. If the cards feel right for you, then they are your cards.

If they do not feel right then simply place these in a safe place as they may actually be for someone you know or maybe they will be used by yourself later in your reading development.

You may find as you develop that you have more than one pack and this too is down to personal preference. Some packs will give a different reading depending on what you or your client is looking for. Again always listen to your instincts on this and choose the appropriate deck for the appropriate reading.

THE TAROT DECK – MINOR ARCANA

The tarot card deck consists of 78 cards and is divided into two sections.

The first of these is the minor Arcana or lesser secrets and consists of 56 cards, divided into four suits of 14 cards each; ten numbered cards and four court cards. The court cards are the King, Queen, Knight and Page/Jack, in each of the four tarot suits.

The tarot suits are Swords, Wands, Pentacles and Cups and when learning Tarot these suits keep their same general categories. The message for each may change but you can use the base for each to start with when doing a reading around these cards.

SUIT OF CUPS

Feelings & Emotions (Family, Relationships, Business relationships, Friends)
Element: Water (Emotions, Opinion, Instinct)

Represented as Hearts in the Playing card deck

Out of the four suits, the Cups seems to be the stumbling block for most people, as there is no real connection between cups and relationships (unlike the other suits below). So this will be the one that you generally have to remember what cups are.

SUIT OF WANDS

Imagination & Creativity (Dreams, Desires, Work, Projects)
Element: Fire (Ambition, Power, Intuition)
Represented as Clubs in the Playing card deck

The wands card is easy to remember by thinking of a magician waving his wand and making dreams and ideas come true.

SUIT OF PENTACLES

Money & Potential (Wealth, Earnings, Funding, Loss, Gain)
Element: Earth (Practical, Grounded, Sensations)
Represented as Diamonds in the Playing card deck

Pentacles look like money, simple as that. When you see the pentacles use the idea of finances and funding as your base for this card.

SUIT OF SWORDS

Life Challenges (Conflicts, Challenges, Troubles, Issues, Concerns)

Element: Air (Concepts, Thinking, Reasoning)

Represented as Spades in the Playing card deck

The swords again you use the idea of going to battle or fighting. This is a good base to use for this card.

As you can see we have not touched on every single card meaning in the minor arcana and there is no need to. Each of the four suites has a specific area they deal with and as long as you remember this for each of the cards then you will not have any issues around it. Just use their base meaning for that card and then you will be able to expand on the given message from there.

You may get a client that wants a reading which touches on relationships, in which case I would only get the client to pick cards out from the Cups suit. Likewise, if a client is more concerned about work then I would use the Wands suit.

It also best not to get too much information from a client prior to the reading as this will dilute the message. Instead of asking what areas of their life you would like to touch on will give you a good idea. Of course, if it seems a little of everything then simply use the whole deck.

THE TAROT DECK - MAJOR ARCANA

Also known as the greater secrete of trump cards, there are 22 cards each without suits and consist of the following cards:

The Magician, The High Priestess, The Empress, The Emperor, The Hierophant, The Lovers, The Chariot, Strength, The Hermit, Wheel of Fortune, Justice, The Hanged Man, Death, Temperance, The Devil, The Tower, The Star, The Moon, The Sun, Judgement, The World and The Fool *(the Fool is represented by the Joker in the playing card deck)*.

Thanks to the likes of Hollywood and their using tarot as a connection to the occult and other dark arts, many of these cards are miss-understood in their meanings and what they are actually about.

Again you do not need to know the literal meaning of each of these cards as this is not how tarot works, and later I will show you an example reading I did with the Chariot card for a client of mine.

There are four cards though that is always not understood or given the right readings because of Hollywood and these are Death, Lovers, The Devil and The Tower.

Each of these I will expand upon so you get an idea of how they interact within a reading.

DEATH CARD

Ever watched a movie where the death card is shown and instantly there is a gasp, shock and even horror on the faces of the actors for the terrors yet to unfold. Who would be the unlucky person who will drop dead at the stroke of midnight?

Well, the answer is no one!

You see the death card has never represented death at all in the tarot deck. It's a representation of change and the new beginnings for the client and is possibly one of the best trump cards to get in a reading.

Yet still, many readers will see this as a negative card and potentially if the person does not want change could be seen as such. I have picked up divorce for example in a Death card which of course would represent change, moving home and even a new career. All these are examples of the representation of changes.

Often I pick up the passing of someone in the Cups suit which would make perfect sense as the Cups card is to do with family and relationships. The trouble is the Death card looks more dramatic than a Cups card on film.

THE LOVERS

Again another huge miss-conception of a card by the film industry is the Lovers card. Instantly you are told that this has to be around Love and finding that special someone.

I remember watching the James Bond movie, Live and Let Die, (released in 1973 and did more harm to the divination of Tarot than any other film), where Bond (Roger Moore), pulls out the Lovers card for the beautiful reader Solitaire (played by Jane Seymour) and instantly she falls into his arms and gives herself to our hero. The problem is if she was a real reader she would have known that this has nothing to do with Lovers.

The card itself has everything to do with passions and making a choice between two or more passions and letting one go. An example of this is if someone likes Shushi and also likes Curry and they are told by the doctor they can only eat one going forward for the rest of the life. Ok, a really bad example, but you get the idea, choice and picking between two things that mean a lot to that person. It can, of course, mean choosing between two people as well.

I remember doing a reading for a lady who got the Lovers card in her spread. She laughed and said that she was 86 and she had not time for a lover in her life (see what I mean). When I explained the actual meaning and then gave her more detail and told her that it was a connection to a home and that she had a choice to leave or stay and that she was, in fact, making the wrong decision in leaving, did she say that the reading for the card was 100% correct.

I personally feel she was a little disappointed that no new young man was coming through!

THE DEVIL

For me, this is one of the most negative cards of all the trump cards in the Tarot deck. It has the representation of repression, anger, sexual pressure, abuse or bounding; being tied to a situation that you are not in control of.

This card would have done well in the movies as it is the one card that truly represents what it is. With this card, you have to be careful how you tread and tends (for myself) to appear in the Past card location of the spreads, but can easily appear as a future card as well (again situations such as divorce).

I have connected and got information about clients that have been hidden or regressed for years, but it's only when these past incidents are exposed does the client actually goes through a period of release and for that reason can then be seen as a positive outcome from a negative card.

Handle this card with care and handle those that get it equally so. Those that are in an abusive relationship (mental or physical) will often get this card in their spreads.

THE TOWER

This card too can (sometimes) come across just as being negative and represents a big change or shift in someone's life. The type of change that will literally move the foundations of their life and can (at times) come with a warning to be heeded.

In one reading, this card appeared in the Past segment of the spread and I was told that the person had a recent death in her family of someone that she was very close too, which would be a huge shift in a person's life.

It transpired that she had, in fact, lost her husband only the previous month to cancer and was still in a very low place.

Of course, a big change could also be positive such as a birth or a new home or even emigration.

What you will discover in this book and when you start to interrupt the cards, the information given so far is really all you ever need when it comes to what I call the base information.

And even if you cannot recall everything simple remember the four minor arcana cards, Cups are relationships, Pentacles is money, Wands is work or dreams and Swords are conflicts.

Even at that minimum base level, you are already well on your way to reading the cards correctly.

LEFT AND RIGHT MEANINGS

In some cards, you will see objects coming from the left or the right-hand side of the card as you look at it. A good example of this is the Ace card within the Minor Arcana. You may even be drawn to a person or object which emphasizes the left or right.

Even on some of the Knight cards, the knight can be seen coming from the left or right, and sometimes the horse's left leg is raised (for example). You do not have to look for these small things, but if you are drawn to the card, and see something from the left or right may have a specific additional meaning for the client.

LEFT MEANING

Anything coming from the left will represents feminine or has to do with the past. The easy way to remember this is that your left arm is closest to your heart (love) for females.

RIGHT MEANING

Anything coming from the right will represent masculine or has to do with the future.

You may even get the feeling the meaning represents both i.e. you see a woman from the past or someone with female energy. Now that may seem strange but with sexual preferences these days it's very easy for you to pick up a male with a lot of female energy which may indicate his sexual preference in society.

My 'gaydar' is not the best if I'm honest and tend to get caught on this a lot (mainly because I have never had any issues with anyone's sexual preferences). In one reading with one young lady, I picked up on a very strong, dominant male energy in her life and told by my guides that this was her partner. What I could not work out is why this partnership with the strong male energy was a female, until my client said that she was in fact gay.

Your indications may be stronger than mine and regardless of your point of view on someone's personal life or the way they feel happy to lead it, you must always respect their decisions and never be judgemental about this.

The same left or right application works with crystal ball too and as you now start to go through the book you will see similar actions apply to both crystal ball and to tarot.

So, for example, you may see in the ball an arrow pointing to the left or maybe even a car pointing to the right. In each case, you apply the base for the left and right meanings accordingly.

SPIRIT GUIDES

I just want to touch on this section before we carry on with working with the tarot and crystal ball.

When doing any form of divination, the tools you use be it tarot, runes, crystals are designed as a tool or marker that you can then ask you guides why has this been given to the client. With Tarot and ball work it's even easier as there are additional meanings throughout that you can use without too much interaction with your guides.

This is why many readings are not specific or too general with the reader taking the literal meaning of the cards and not using their guides to provide a full define reading. To put it simply divination is used for channeling and that is all.

But I hear you say, I do not have a connection with my guides or I cannot hear them!

This is where you will use the instincts of your gut instincts for doing the readings as our guides tend to use these when we do not have the ability to hear them.

One word of advice, whatever you feel first in your gut is normally the right thing. The biggest traps readers will fall into is over-thinking the cards, second-guessing or even self-doubt.

If you are looking to develop your Psychic connections or your connection with your spirit guides, then I suggest that you consider taking my online Psychic development course.

Contact me directly via my website (www.markhoward.co.za) and let me know you have purchased this book. I will be more than happy to give you 50% off the advertised price of the course.

PREPARING FOR A READING

Preparation is so important for any reading. Sometimes it's not possible, especially if doing a group reading or someone asks you out of the blue to do one. I recall when I first started to do readings at fayres and I thought what on earth has I gotten into?

The thing is you can do as much or as little as you want in preparation, and the more you do the better the reading.

Two important things to remember about the following. You should use this as much as you can for both tarot and ball readings and also this can be used for distance readings as well. I suggest when you first start to use these as a guideline and as you develop and grow into the readings that you work with those sections that work best for you.

- Meditate the day before the reading. Connect with your client (you just need their first name only) and ask your Spirit Guide(s) to come forward. If you are not aware of your guides, then please use your intuition for the readings, but asking for them to come forward will also help you to develop a connection with them over a period of time.

- Make a note of any images, smells, intuition, even pains that you get. You do not need to write these down as your Spirit Guide(s) will bring these back to you during the reading IF they are relevant at that time.

- NO alcohol or caffeine at least 2 hours before the reading or during the reading and it is advisable to stick to water. This is not because if any dangers other than alcohol tend to loosen your tongue and that you may actually be the way to open during the reading.

- Have a comfortable place to sit, for you and your client. On the table have a lighted white candle (Spirit are drawn to white candles)

- A box of tissues handy nearby. You will need these and the number of times I have not put out tissues and asked clients if they want them to be told no, only to find they are in floods of tears at the end of the first card.

- Your tarot cloth for the cards to be placed upon during the reading.

- Glasses of water for you and your client.

WHEN YOUR CLIENT SITS FOR THE READING

Unless your client has had a reading before, then for many this will be a nerve-racking time. After all, they do not know what to expect and (in most cases) will already have pre-conceived ideas.

For this reason, it is important that you talk with your client first to understand what it is they are looking for from a reading. Is it a general reading or do they have specific questions that they would like to be answered?

In the case of the latter its best if the client does NOT give their questions to start with as this will dilute the reading. Instead, advise the client that any questions they have can be asked at the end of the reading.

I tend to start by going through the code of ethics of which there is an example that I use below. It's a bit like a doctor/patient confidentiality verbal agreement between you and your client. Remember, if they have never had a reading before, the chances are they will be nervous and this is a great opportunity to calm them down and to allow them to open up.

EXAMPLE CODE OF ETHICS

The following is the code of ethics I use with all my students and all my clients. You will be surprised how many readers do NOT have any form of code of ethics which shows lack of training and respect for their clients

- You can only give them what has been given to you by your Spirit Guide(s). If you are not meant to know something or it's not relevant at that time, it will not be given.

- What is said in the room is between you and them only. If the client wants to repeat what was said to friends afterward that's up to them

- If something is given which the client does not know or understand just ask them to accept it as it might mean something later on.

- If at any point the client wishes to stop the reading they can do so. Simply close down the reading and bring the session to a close.

- If they are not sure of anything, have a question or need clarification during the reading, remind them to just ask. The reading is for them and will (hopefully) be a great experience for them.

- If the client wants to record the reading or take notes, allow them. It adds to your credibility and also will help the client days later when they want to refer back to the reading.

- Tell them the more open they are and relaxed, the better the reading will be.

Finally, advise that you tend to keep your eyes closed during the readings. This may sound strange but there is a solid reason for doing this. Once you have the card turned over, look at the card and then close your eyes and visualize the card (this helps with third eye development too) and give the reading for that card. You may need to quickly open your eyes and re-look at the card then do so.

The reason you do this is that most readers can pick up body language from their clients. This can, in fact, be off-putting of even give you miss-signals from your client as you are doing the reading. The common one for this is when you are doing the reading the client looks confused and then your self-doubt creeps in. Often clients look confused as they are trying to fathom out where that part of the reading is going and once you have completed it, a light bulb goes on and they confirm or understand what is being said.

By closing your eyes you are shutting this off and allows you to concentrate on the card reading 100% without distractions.

In one reading I had two ladies approach me and one asked for a reading, which I was more than happy to do. During the reading, she was stone-faced! Not a single emotion, flicker nothing came through and the first thought I had was that I would never want to play poker against this woman.

I carried on the reading like this all the way through with not a word from my client until the end, at which point she thanked me and walked off.

About half an hour later her friend came over and asked me for reading as well as her friend said it was the best and most accurate reading she ever had.

It goes to show that you need to trust in what is being given and close your eyes – it will help so much in your development and how you do your readings.

STARTING A READING - PREPARING THE CARDS

Chances are, your cards will have yours or someone else's energy on them. You will need to cleanse the cards and get the clients' energy onto them. This can be a great way to calm the client down.

I actually overheard one 'reader' advise another that cleansing the cards is a waste of time. Like all good tradespeople, if you do not look after your tools, then how do you expect your tools to do the right job for you? So you will need to cleanse the cards for every single reading.

One last thought on energies. If you wear rings, a wedding band of a watch, then you should remove these are these will have your energies and (in the case of the wedding band), energies of other people as well – I have termed this procedure as "Getting Naked for Tarot".

1. Tell your client you are going to cleanse the cards.

2. Ask them to close their eyes and relax. Breathing gently in and out whilst they listen to you cleanse the

cards. You can also run a quick breathing exercise where they breathe in positivity and breath out negativity

3. Shuffle the cards yourself before you start the cleansing. I used to get clients to do this but found may do not know how to shuffle and would actually damage the cards in their attempts,

4. One by one, place each card (face down) onto the table and as you do so; in your head say "Clean" or "Cleanse". This does not have to take a huge amount of time and when you are up to speed this process so takes no longer than around 1 to 2 minutes.

5. When you have finished, place the deck in front of your client and ask them to open their eyes.

Your client is now ready to begin choosing their cards.

Ask the client to hold the deck in both hands and close their eyes. Ask them to imagine their energy running from one hand, through the deck to the other hand and back again (give them about 1 minute or when you feel they are ready).

Whilst your client is relaxing and placing their energies onto the cards, there are a number of points you will need to run through.

- *Ask your Spirit Guide(s) to join you for the reading and to give you confirmation that they are with you. You may feel a light touch on your head or even a voice. Even if you do not feel or hear anything please do this as a matter of course.*

- *Imagine an umbilical cord going from your navel, round your back via your left-hand side, back to the front of you and then around your clients' opposite side (right hand), around their back and back to their front (left hand) and connect to their navel. You are now linked with your client. (see Connecting with your Client below)*

- *Open your chakras fully; starting with your root chakra and finishing with your crown chakra. If you are not aware of your chakras I have outlined these on the next few pages and included a good diagram to help you at the rear of this book. You can also open your chakras before your client arrives and close at the end of the day if you are having a number of clients that you are reading for.*

• *Ask your Spirit Guide(s) if you should use the full deck or if it's to be split. If split which deck would be chosen? The one on the left or right? (Once the pack has been split). Again if you are not connected fully to your guides always go with your instincts.*

1. If the deck is to be split ask the client to split the deck and take the pile your Spirit Guide(s) tell you too.

2. I would advise you to spread the cards out, face down, as best as possible. Again I used to get clients to do this and again many cannot spread a deck of cards without damaging the cards.

3. Ask the client to look over the cards to pick the cards they are drawn to. The must choose the number of cards as per the spread you will be doing for them. Some clients will want to place their hands over the cards to sense the energy which is perfectly fine. I

even had one person use his lottery numbers to pick
the cards and still had one of the best readings I know.

4. Each card must place them face down, on top of each
    other. So card 1 will be at the bottom of the pile with
    the last card picked at the top.

5. Collect the unused cards and put them to one side;
    give them love and light.

6. Collect the chosen cards, face down, in a pile to start
    the client's reading.

HOW TO CONNECT WITH YOUR CLIENT

Once you are ready remember to connect with your client by creating an umbilical cord that does a figure 8 between you and your client (as described above).

Many readers do not even carry out this practice which then asks the question of how they are even working with their client.

You can also connect to any person regardless of their location. This is ideal if you are doing distance readings and you only need the person's first name. Some readers will ask for the date of birth as well but this really is not necessary.

You can also connect to people in a social environment as well in this manner but just be careful, as once you are connected you will start to see images and get a lot about the person the second you connect.

It is also worth noting that the hardest people to connect to are men (in general) and other light-workers. I accidentally connected to a well-known UK spiritual medium some years back without even realizing it. She, however, did know and she came through to my third eye very quickly to find out who I was – so again be careful who you decide to connect with

When you have completed the reading, remember to disconnect my visualizing a pair of scissors cutting the cord and then asking Archangel Michael to help heal and seal the ends.

WHAT ARE YOUR CHAKRAS AND HOW TO OPEN THEM!

Even if you are fully aware of your chakras and how to use them, I strongly suggest reading this section of the book, as I cover a lot taken from my Psychic Development class on how you can use your Chakras effectively.

Chakras are the concentrated energy centers of the body. Chakra is a Sanskrit term and it means "wheel" or "disk" and is derived from the root word "cakra". Chakras are spinning wheels of energy/light.

There are seven main chakras that we will be concentrating on and these start with your root chakra (red) which is located at the base of your spine and then proceeds up to your crown chakra (white) which is located on the crown of your head.

If you imagine each chakra as a spinning disk of light each spinning clockwise then you will be on the right track.

The seven main chakras are represented as follows:

ROOT CHAKRA

This chakra's role is to connect all of your energy with the Earth, which is called grounding.

COLOUR: RED

Location: This chakra is located at the very base of your spine, near your tailbone. It goes up to just below your belly button.

UNBALANCED

You may experience frequent daydreaming, trouble concentrating or simply feeling like your "head's in the clouds." People may say you appear "airheaded" or "spacey."

SACRAL CHAKRA

Your sacral chakra is the home of the creative life force energy that helps you enjoy your life here on Earth.

It's the energy that motivates you to enjoy the fruits of your labor including indulging in pleasurable activities like sex. Also known for creativity.

COLOUR: ORANGE

Location: The sacral chakra is located right below the belly button and extends to its center.

UNBALANCED

This chakra is often overactive when we face things like addiction and gluttony. Pleasure is a good thing, and you should never feel guilty for enjoying the good things life has to offer.

SOLAR PLEXUS

This chakra is where your self-confidence, identity, and personal power are born. Iy also where our guides may initially connect with us on a personal level when there are issues – you may have heard of the phrase "gut instinct" for example.

COLOUR: YELLOW

Location: The solar plexus starts in the center of the belly button and extends up to the breastbone or where your two sets of ribs connect in the center of your chest.

UNBALANCED

You may feel quick to anger, the need to control and micromanage, greediness and a lack of compassion or empathy.

HEART

This chakra is where your love, compassion, and kindness are empowered.

This includes love for others and love for yourself, which is why this chakra is also associated with health

COLOUR: GREEN

Location: The heart chakra's center is located right over your heart and it radiates down to your breastbone and up to your throat.

UNBALANCED

You may find yourself always putting the needs of others before your own.

Symptoms include a fast heart rate, palpitations, heartburn and interpersonal relationship issues.

THROAT

This chakra gives a voice to your personal truths. This chakra lets you speak your truth with clarity. Resting right above the heart, the throat chakra is connected to the compassion and love you have for yourself and others.

COLOUR: BLUE

Location: The throat chakra's center is right in between your collar bone, and it radiates down to the center of your heart and up to the center of your eyes.

UNBALANCED

Will often interrupt others, often be told they have a loud voice or "love to hear themselves talk." Physically, you may suffer from throat pain, frequent infections, cavities or mouth ulcers.

THIRD EYE

This chakra opens up your mind to information beyond the

material world and the 5 senses. Extrasensory perception, intuition or psychic energy, all comes from the third eye. When people use the word "Clairvoyant" they are actually talking about the third eye.

COLOUR: INDIGO OR PURPLE

Location: The third eye's center is in between your eyebrows. It radiates down to your mouth and up to the top of your head.

CROWN

This chakra is pure consciousness energy. It is our connection to the spirit world to loved ones who have passed and to our guides.

COLOUR: VIOLET - WHITE

Location: The crown chakra's center is at the top of your head. It radiates down to between your eyes and then extends infinitely upward and outward, connecting you to the energy of the rest of the universe.

When opening your chakras you always start with your root and make your way to the crown chakra. Imagine for each chakra lotus petals around them and you are opening these up to allow the chakra color to shine through.

Likewise at the end to close your chakras you start with your crown and work to your root. Again you visualize the lotus petals closing around each chakra until only a pinprick of light is coming through.

If you would like my guided chakra cleaning mediation you can download this for free at - **http://bit.ly/2SKppOz**

HOW TO EMPHASIS YOU CHAKRAS

There may be a time when you need to emphasis or "boost" your chakras depending on what you want or need to be doing.

By wearing accessories, clothing or even items such as jewelry in the color of one of the chakras will help to "boost" that chakra for you

A good example of this is that politicians or those doing public speaking will tend to wear blue or have blue accessories around them. Those that work in the arts, writing, and music and so on will tend to have a lot of orange around them.

If you do not have an item of that color then something simple as a pin badge is as good. I sometimes wear a red band on my wrist when I need grounding during a reading.

GROUNDING DURING THE READING.

It is very important that you are ground during the reading and afterward as well. One of the easiest ways is to remove your shoes and socks and complete the reading barefoot. Strange I know and but this really helps with the grounding and ensures are great reading.

When you complete the reading you will also need to ground (after you have closed your chakras) and for this, I suggest you download my grounding guided meditation which will take you through this - **http://bit.ly/2TBk8Zy**

PLACING THE CARDS FOR THE READING

When you start to place down the cards for the reading there are two ways you can do this:

1. Place the cards (starting with the top card) into the spread formation and turn each card over one-by-one once you have finished reading each card in turn.

2. Place the first card down and when you have completed reading the card place the next card; read it and continue until you have completed the spread formation.

3. When you are reading the cards, sometimes a card will be laid facing upside down to yourself. Some readers will tell you that this gives the opposite meaning or negative meaning to that card – these people are taking the literal meaning of the cards and this is not Tarot reading. If this happens, turn the card the correct way towards you and continue the reading.

4. Do not place all the cards face up into the spread formation and then start the reading. This distracts you and your client form the cards you are reading at that time

Over time you will become comfortable with your own way of doing the spreads and how you want to lay out the cards. As your development grows and your connection with your guides grows you will start to find that cards that are placed in a position on a spread are not that defined position. An example of this is that for me, more often than not, the card sitting in the Past card position is not a representation of the past but could be an indication for another time period or even future event.

I have also found that my guides will sometimes ask to be to get the client to pick a different number of cads as opposed to the spread that I will be doing. In this case, they will then advise how they want me to lay the cards out for that reading.

On a side note to this, you may find your client picks an additional card to the number you need for the spread. So, for example, they may pick six cards not five for the five-card spread (as shown in this book). In this case, still read the card but place the sixth (or even seventh) card last and where you feel it needs to be placed in the spread – you really cannot go too wrong.

14 TAROT SPREADS YOU CAN START USING TODAY!

SINGLE CARD SPREADS

The single card draw is best for times when you want to focus on one thing without any potential complications.

It can be used for just about any question you can ask, including to draw a card of the day, week, or even your ultimate destiny.

It can also be used in succession, as some readers like to pull one card at a time as a story unfolds. Some readers don't even like to use actual spreads, relying on this method alone.

I have also used this spread for giving readings on the radio, but it's difficult to give these readings, as the stations do not want and 'dead' air and you need to keep talking all the way through until you get the information you need.

Where I advise my students to use this card is when you want to give yourself a daily reading or get a quick, personal answer to a situation you may be going through at that time.

PAST, PRESENT AND FUTURE

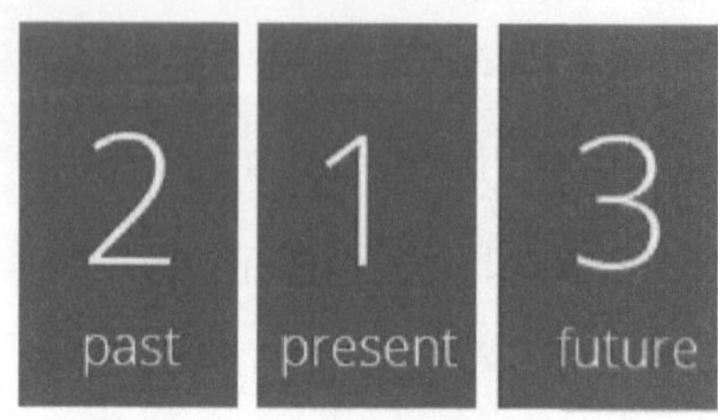

This simplistic chronological spread can be used to shed light on the influences that are now behind you, current influences, and what is approaching in the near future.

Not much explanation is necessary on this one. Since anyone can understand this spread, it can be found on practically every tarot reading site and instruction book.

The important aspect to remember as that card one if off the TOP of the pile and not off the bottom, card two is the middle card and card 3 the last card on the bottom (which would have been the first card picked by the client).

So, in essence, you are laying out the cards in the reverse order that they were picked by your client.

This is important to understand as this process is the same for each of the following spreads going forward.

THE BLIND SPOT

This spread is used to enhance self-awareness.

Questions about learning something about yourself or things that are hidden, work very well with this spread, but actually, no question is necessary.

1. This card displays the obvious identity, the part of yourself that you are consciously aware of and project to others.

2. This card shows unconscious driving forces that neither you nor others are aware of about you. This is the Great Unknown. Nobody knows what this card means.

3. The part of yourself that you conceal, that you don't want others to know about is apparent in this card.

4. This is your Blind Spot. This is what you asked about which you should be made aware of by this reading. You may wish to pay close attention to these mannerisms.

THE CROSS

The Cross Spread is good for questions asking for advice. It can also be used to determine the meaning of a confusing card from a previous reading, or for that matter, to shed light on other points of confusion as well.

In questions asking advice, this spread is self-explanatory. The main thing is to determine the difference between cards #2 and #3. #1 is the topic and #4 is the result.

In questions regarding confusion, such as: "What was the meaning of Card (X) in the last spread?" The main thing is also to determine the difference between cards #2 and #3.

In this case, Card #2 will show what the card was not referring to, and Card #3 will show what the card really meant. #1 is the topic and #4 represents the purpose it serves.

THE HORSE SHOE

The Horse Shoe is an old classic tarot spread. It is more advanced than the 3-card reading, yet simpler than most other spreads. It is a versatile method that can be used for most queries, though there are other spreads that would go into more depth.

Like the simple Past, Present, and Future spread, it contains these cards in positions 1, 2, and 7, but also has 4 other cards that help the reader understand how to deal with the Future better. The cards are to be read as follows:

1. The Past: This card represents past events that are affecting the question.

2. The Present: This card represents the current state or immediately approaching influence.

3. Hidden Influences: Things that you may not be aware of, or barely be aware of.

4. Obstacles: This is the challenge. Obstacles might be avoided, or you may have to deal with them.

5. External Influences: Attitudes and thoughts about this situation from people.

6. Suggestions: Recommended course of action.

7. The Final Outcome: This card represents what would happen if the suggestion is followed.

THE CELTIC CROSS

This is probably the most common spread. A good basic spread for beginners to use for practice, the Celtic Cross is useful for questions of all types. In this spread it can be helpful to notice the relationships between the pairings of cards #5 & #9, #1 & #2, #3 & #4, and #6 & #10.

1. The significate shows what the reading deals with, the initial situation.

2. An added impulse that compounds the significate, which may be either complementary or contradictory.

3. This is what the client is consciously aware of (thoughts).

4. Unconscious driving forces the client may not be aware of (emotions).

5. The immediate past regarding the current situation.

6. The first future card indicates the immediate future.

7. This card represents the client and their attitude towards cards #1 and #2.

8. The external influences, the places and people that influence the topic.

9. This card is the client's expectations; what is secretly hoped for or feared.

10. The second future card shows the longer-term outcome.

THE SECRET OF THE HIGH PRIESTESS

This spread is a nice alternative to the Celtic Cross, which covers basically the same ground. It is useful when a question doesn't quite call for the Ankh spread. This spread is helpful when you are looking into a current trend. The High Priestess may or may not present a mysterious secret to be analyzed after the rest of the spread.

1. and 2. Main impulses that represent the topic at hand. They may complement or oppose one another.

3. This is the current influence at this time.

5. The Waning Moon is the influence that you are putting behind you, what is moving into the past.

4. The Waxing Moon indicates what is on the horizon, or the approaching influence. This is the immediate future.

7. The Light is what is clearly recognized, what is conscious.

6. The Dark shows what is there but not fully perceived, though noticed on a deeper level of consciousness.

8. The Next Step is the near future, where this journey will take you.

9. The last card, if it happens to be of the Major Arcana, reveals the Secret of the High Priestess. This is a special message that you should pay extra special attention to.

RELATIONSHIP – VERSION ONE

This spread is easy to read, like a convenient chart. In this spread, court cards generally indicate actual people with the same characteristics. Knights (or corresponding Princes, but not Kings) and Queens are meant to represent actual men and women in this tarot spread. Look for patterns in the cards as always.

Card #1 is the overall signification of the relationship. The 2 columns on either side of the signification characterize each individual's role in the relationship. The relationship does not have to be romantic. In fact, it could be a relationship between a person and a group, or even how 2 groups relate.

The top row, cards #7 & 2, shows the conscious thoughts of each person, or what they think about the relationship and likewise how they view their partner.

The middle row, cards #6 & 3, shows the way each individual feels about the other. Emotional awareness corresponds to a person's unconscious thoughts that run deep, affecting a person in ways he or she is not fully aware of.

The bottom row, cards #5 & 4, represents the way each person behaves, in other words, the stance taken regarding the relationship. The way a person acts may be genuine, but sometimes people are phony and manipulative, so it is best to weigh this card against your partner's other cards to determine if they match up.

RELATIONSHIP – VERSION TWO

This relationship spread focuses more on the common ground of the relationship, with 3 cards in the middle column showing the common ground. The middle column essentially shows the past, present, and future of the relationship.

Card #4 shows the common base of the relationship, which may be thought of as the past events which have shaped their characters, bringing them together. Card #3 represents the current connection that binds them together, the values they share. Card #7 shows the common goals that would keep them together moving into the future.

The columns on either side show what each partner brings to the table. Remember, relationships need not be romantic, and the partners could even be groups rather than individuals, whatever you choose. In this layout, the other person is on the left-hand side, and you, the client on the right.

Cards #1 & 2 indicate the separate personalities of each member of the relationship. These cards form a sort of bridge with the cards beneath them, #5 & 6, which show the qualities that each partner offers the other person, and thus to the relationship as a whole.

THE DECISION

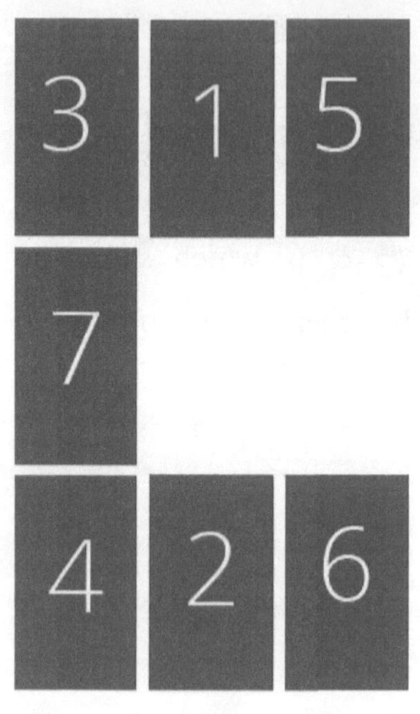

This simple but highly useful spread calls for a question to be asked in this format:

"What happens if I do (X), and what happens if I do not do (X)?"

Please note that it should not be viewed as a decision between 2 different options, but about whether or not a single option should be exercised. A second option would call for a separate reading.

Card #7 is the significator, the overall theme of the query.

Cards #3, #1, & #5 represent the chronological sequence of events that occurs if you choose to do (X).

Cards #4, #2, & #6 represent the chronological sequence of events that unfolds if you choose NOT to do (X).

THE PATH

For the Path, the client asks for suggestions on how to behave properly in order to achieve the desired result. The Current column (cards 2,3,4) shows how the client has been acting, and the Suggested column (cards 5,6,7) suggests how the client should act in order to achieve a certain goal. The chart-like spread uses the standard 3 levels: Rational, Emotional, and External Stance (how one projects one's self outwardly). When comparing the Current to Suggested cards, the most important thing is to notice the differences between the 2 cards. It is these differences that hint at the behaviors that you should think about changing.

Card #1 is the significator, the card which should reflect the nature of the query and/or the desired outcome.

Card #2 shows the way you are and have been thinking. Card #7 shows how you need to change the way you think in order to serve yourself better.

Card #3 tells you about your emotional attitude. Though it may seem difficult to manipulate one's own emotions, it can be done if you put your mind to it. For example, acting a certain way such as smiling intently for a few minutes will lead the emotions to follow. If you try this, as silly as the exercise seems, you will find that this evokes the emotion of happiness. For this reading, you should try to make yourself feel the way that Card #6 tells you.

External Stance means how you act outwardly, how you hope others see you. Card #4 tells you how you were acting, while #5 indicates how you should act outwardly, for other people's sake. It is the differences between these cards that hint at what behavior patterns should be altered.

THE GAME PLAN

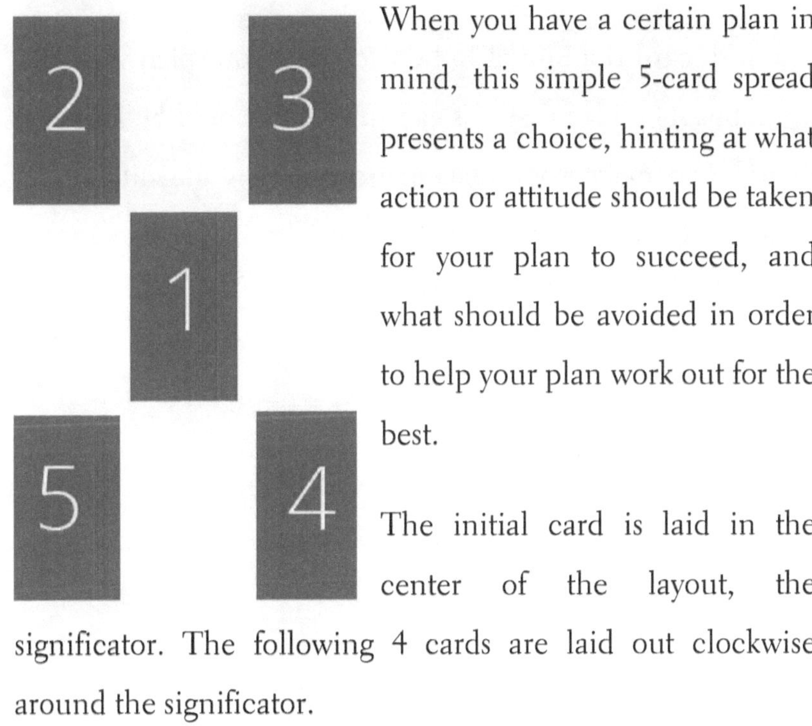

When you have a certain plan in mind, this simple 5-card spread presents a choice, hinting at what action or attitude should be taken for your plan to succeed, and what should be avoided in order to help your plan work out for the best.

The initial card is laid in the center of the layout, the significator. The following 4 cards are laid out clockwise around the significator.

In this spread, the second card shows what drives you, but also says you are not fully conscious of this, perhaps even completely unaware of it. It gives you a hint as to the reason that you strive for your goal.

The third card shows what others think of you and your goals. You may or may not be aware of this. Sometimes other people factor into your plans, and sometimes they don't.

The fourth card shows what you should not do. If things are permitted to go down this path, your plan will collapse.

The fifth card is a hint as to how to make your plan work out favorably. The idea that this card presents should be followed in order to make your plan a success. It is the differences between Cards #4 and #5 that should be noted, as the differences provide the clues you need.

THE HOWARD SPREAD

This spread has a special significance as this was given to me by my Spirit Guides as a way to do a year's reading without using too much energy. You are welcome to use this spread.

All I ask is that you call this the "Howard Spread" in respect.

This is the spread I personally use and what I like about it is that; by the time you have read Card 2, you will have given your client a lot of confirmation before you start with the future cards.

Card 1 – The Present or theme

Card 2 – The Past

Card 3 – General up to 6 months

Card 4 – Affirmation card or answer to the question.

Card 5 – General 6 to 12 months

Card 6 – 0 to 3 months

Card 7 – 3 to 6 months

Card 8 – 6 to 9 months

Card 9 – 9 to 12 months

Card 3 (the Past) I have found now does not always represent the past or even influences on the past and can sometimes give a general-purpose to the reading and of information related to future events.

Again you need to use your instincts or ask your guides when you get to this card.

THE FIVE CARD SPREAD

This spread is great for both general readings and answers to a question or problem.

This is the spread I teach my students to use and master first; as with the Howard Spread, by the time you have read Card 2, you will have given your client a lot of confirmation and evidential information which helps with the remainder of the reading.

It is also a great spread when doing email readings or distance readings for a client

Card 1 – The Present or theme

Card 2 – The Past

Card 3 – General Future

Card 4 – Answer to the question

Card 5 – Solution to the Problem

READING THE CARDS

So far we have covered the following:

1. Minor and Major arcana cards and their base meanings
2. Preparation
3. Card spreads

You are now ready to start the process of reading a card(s) for your client and this can actually be the easiest part. You just need to trust your instincts (guides) and go with what you feel you are being drawn to.

One of the issues with a lot of "tarot readers" is that they have been trained to read the cards as their literal meaning, which is not what tarot is about. Remember this is a tool to be used between yourself and your Spirit Guide(s) to give clear and concise readings to your client.

In some cases, you might give the literal meaning for the client if that's what your Spirit Guide(s) tells you. Either way, you need to listen and build your relationship with your Spirit Guide(s).

Reading the cards takes a lot of energy and concentration. You need to use all your senses, touch, taste, smell, sight (third eye) and hearing (guides)

1. Note where the card is placed within the spread, is it in the past card location or the future card location i.e. the next 6 months. This will give you an indication of timeframes for that card.

2. Look at the card carefully and ask your Spirit Guide(s) why this card has been chosen for the client

3. If it's a minor arcana use the base meaning i.e. for Cups use the relationships, family and so on

4. What areas of the card are you drawn to?

    Is it a color, an object or a symbol?
    Again ask your guide(s) why you are being drawn to these specific things.

5. Relate colors to the Chakras so Red, for example, may mean grounding is required. A lack of color may mean a lack of something

i.e. a lack of Blue may relate to communication issues. Again ask where is the communication issue? How will it occur?

I tend to use Black for negativity or problems and White for Spirit.

6. Again use the literal meaning as a base and talk to your Spirit Guide(s).

"I know that this card means this but is that for the client?"

7. Ask your Spirit Guide(s) if there is anything on the card that you should be drawn to and if so, why?

8. Is there something you are NOT seeing? Sometimes an image or object removed may indicate something missing in the person's life

9. Remember the Left and Right we spoke about at the start of this book? With left being Female and the past and right being Male and the future.

10. Use your senses at all times – I even got a sense of mint in my mouth at one reading which indicated that the person was concerned about her mother who was always eating mints.

11. Keep your eyes closed and use your third eye. Images that come through your third eye will have a meaning for your client.

It might sound like a lot of work but as you do more and more readings, you will find it easier, and the connection with your Spirit Guide(s) will become stronger as you go along.

Again you will start to develop your own ways of reading certain cards and get a sense of what is being given. Trust your instincts as they will always be correct.

In one reading I was seeing a lot of Pyramids and getting a lot of images relating to Egypt. When I mentioned this to my client she confirmed that her dad was, in fact, Egyptian and she had been worried about him recently.

In another, I was given a specific year for the client and advised that the year 1984 held a strong and special meaning for her. In this case, the client said that it had nothing to do with her and that she was born in 1982.

I replied that it had nothing to do with her birth but was an indication that this was a special year. She said it did not and in cases like this move on with the reading.

Clients will try to overthink the reading and will not understand everything you give them and it is best to just ask them to take it away as it might mean something later. This is another pit full and does put self-doubt into you but you must continue with the reading and put it to one side.

In this case, the client called me the following morning to apologize. It turned out in 1984 was a very special year for her as it was the year she was adopted!

It is important at this part that you are at least aware of another potential area that needs to be handled with care and attention.

When working with the client and especially when you are connected to them, you will start to get a lot of information and I mean *information*. If someone is having an affair, for example, thinking of leaving their partner or even if their partner is thinking of leaving them.

These areas need to be handled with caution and asking questions such as "how are things at home?" or "so how are things with the family?" will give you an indication if the person is aware or not.

In one reading it became apparent that the client's husband was being unfaithful to her. So I decided to approach the subject by suggesting that there were a barrier and distance between her and her husband at that time.

She confirmed that not only was he being unfaithful, so was she – at least I got the confirmation from the reading first though!

EXAMPLE CARD READING

I like to use the following with my students as an idea of how a card can be read when you are with a client. In this reading the card picked was the Chariot (major arcana) and was in the Present or current location of the spread.

The first thing I noticed was that the two horses are pulling me in two different directions. The black horse one way and the white horse the other. I also felt out of control and not sure of where or what I should be doing.

The black horse I was told was a male manager (so now I know this is related to work) and the white horse a female colleague who has more authority than my client but is the same level.

Next, I noted that there were a lot of blacks (negativity) around her but this started to get smaller as I looked at the card. I also noted the lack of red (grounding) within the card itself.

Finally, I noted that as I looked at the blue color (communication) it went out of focus and back in focus.

The reading as follows:

"You are currently having some big issues at work which is giving you stress and making you feel down, the good news is this will soon become easier as the problem you are having is between two people. The first is your manager who is a man and is telling you to do one thing. The second is a supervisor who is a female who is telling you to do the opposite and you really are not sure what you should be doing.

The problem is the lack of communication between the two and you need to be more focused on what you know you should be doing rather than listening to these two people. Speak with the manager and make them aware of the situation and this will reduce the negativity and bring back positivity into your working environment"

All this from listening and looking at the card. My client confirmed what I had said was 100% correct and she will indeed talk to her manager.

SPIRITS AND LOVED ONES DURING THE READING

Sometimes Spirit may come through for a client during the reading and will make themselves known to you. This tends to be more nerve-wracking for the client than for you and should be handled as gently as possible.

If Spirit come through acknowledge them straight away and ask them who they are. They may or may not give you a name. They might show themselves instead.

Stop the reading and advise the client if a Spirit has come through and given the client any information that is given to you by the Spirit or via your Spirit guide(s).

Remember Spirit use their birth names, not the nicknames that they had. An example of this is a Spirit may say his name is Robert and your client may say they do not know Robert. Chances are they had an Uncle Bob though (Bob is shortened from Robert).

When done, thank the Spirit, give them love and light and continue with the reading.

Note that in my personal experience (unless I'm specifically bringing Spirit through) most passed loved ones really only want to say Hello and just say how much they are missing the person and talk about past events. The same as any loved would do in a general conversation. It is always worth asking Spirit to give some kind of evidential wording for your client.

This will vary from person to person, and for me, I tend to see the loved one and am able to give a detailed description of them. Sometimes they will give me pain and indicate to me how they passed.

For you, working with Spirit will be different and is something you need to work closely with your guide(s) and draw up guidelines that you both agree upon when working with Spirit.

I'm not going to touch on channeling in this book and if this is something you are uncomfortable with at this time, just ask your guides to prevent anyone coming through and this will be fine.

CLOSING AND READING

Once you have completed your clients reading please make sure they are ok. Ask them if they would like you to clarify any part of the reading back to them.

As an added value I tend to take a photo of the spread which I then send to them on email so they have something to refer back too later.

If all is completed then you need to carry out the final sections to close the reading.

- Give Love and Light to the cards and wrap them back into their silk ready for the next reading. If you have a number of readings you may want to consider cleansing the cards ready for the next client as well.

- Unlink from your client. To do this imagine taking some scissors and cutting the umbilical cord that you created when you first linked up at the start of the reading. I tend to ask Archangel Michael to then bless and heal the cord ends.

- Close your chakras. Starting with your crown chakra imagine a lotus leaf closing around each one until only a pinprick of light is visible from each one. Do this until you get to your root chakra (please see the section on chakras in this book)

- When your client has left carryout a grounding meditation/exercise.

Most clients will not give feedback or they may come back sometime in the future with confirmation on the reading. Again learn from each reading you do and ensure your clients are always happy and comfortable.

There are, however, times when you do not want to do a reading for someone or you start reading and you do not feel comfortable with the client. It does happen and in these cases just advise the client you are not ready to do their reading and advise you will contact them later (also do not take payment for readings you decide to cancel or stop).

With one person, she came to me and wanted to hear how she and a guy she had been seeing would end up together and get married. By the second card, it was evident that this was not the case and the client became abusive and angry.

She even said how another reader advised that they would get together.

The thing is you should give what is given – the good and the bad. If a client wants the reading "sugar-coated" tell them to go elsewhere as this is not how readings work.

I calmly advised that I was no longer happy to do the reading and asked her to leave. Another lady came in and was very rude to me before we even started and even started to slag off my wife. Again I asked her to leave and never to ask me for reading again.

She then decided to apologize and pamper to my ego by trying to get me to do her reading. Never let your ego get the better of you and simply walk away. These people are not your clients and they can wherever they want, just not with you.

Never be afraid to cancel a reading. What's more, if you are unwell then please ensure you re-arrange the reading with your client.

And finally, never get put out that people use different readers. The right person will come to you. Some will prefer your style and others will prefer a different person.

CRYSTAL BALL READINGS

INTRODUCTION TO CRYSTAL BALL

As with tarot card reading, crystal ball reading will tend to follow many of the same principles for readings which makes working with both tarot and crystal ball a great way to provide and give information for your clients.

Many people ask me what is the main difference between say Tarot and Crystal ball readings and my reply is simply this – **if tarot reading is Morse code, then crystal ball is video calling.**

A huge difference between the two and it is only when you start to work with your crystal ball do you get to understand the differences between the two.

As with all divination tools that you can use, one of the great things I have found that you can use both Tarot and Ball reading in conjunction with each other.

Although it is possible to use a Ball reading for general readings for a client, I have found that using this for more specific questions has proven to more powerful.

You can also use crystal balls for finding lost objects, animals, and help with the location of someone – basically, anything the client requires can be done through the ball.

When I first started on this the hardest part I found was determine what the symbols mean as there is each will symbol would mean something to you so for example if you see an apple it may mean something each time. The important aspect again is to use this as a connection with your guides and use it as a form of channeling.

I have listed out in this book some of the objects I have seen and personally been able to associate with behind their meanings.

An example of this was reading for one client I picked what looked like a car but as I watched this seems to look more like an SUV of some kind and was given that this was a land rover. I was also told that the color was white (note you will not be able to determine colors directly in the crystal ball) and that the client should be careful of the owner of this car.

The client confirmed that recently a new neighbor with a white Landrover had moved into the area and was causing a lot of issues and bad feelings in the neighborhood. Turned out he was a drug dealer trying to intimidate his neighbors.

I often get asked if I see people in the crystal ball as well such as a "tall dark stranger" which you will (again) find in movies.

The fact is you will see people in the crystal ball and you will get a sense of what they look like (size, build and so on) and even what they are wearing i.e. glasses, hats, etc.

As you develop your reading skills you will even see people in the crystal ball talking and moving around – yes I know that is strange and even the first time I saw this I thought I was going mad.

The point is, working with a crystal ball will give you so much more and you will find that you will have a preference for working in this medium over tarot for example in the future.

CHOOSING YOUR CRYSTAL BALL

One of the biggest mistakes people make with choosing their ball is that they go for a totally clear crystal – maybe this is a knockback due to films portraying crystal ball readers using such, but in fact, this is not the ideal ball to purchase.

You need to find a ball that has imperfections in them. The more the better ideally but not too much that these imperfections merge or look "misty" to you – in fact, some clearness is good so a combination of the two will work well.

The advantage is this makes reading the ball a lot easier and has the added benefit that balls with more imperfections in them are cheaper than those without (but don't tell that to the shops or they will up their prices).

I tend to have a number of crystals that I like and hold them in my hands and choose the one I'm drawn too. I often will look through the ball and see how the imperfections are and how easy it is to read.

Avoid glass balls and keep to the crystal for your first one, but this does not mean you need to stay with this and once you start to get confident you can use different types of balls for different reading options:

Birthstones – ideal for reading someone based on the birth or even for reading during that month i.e. March would be a red crystal.

Health – this is always a tricky subject and one we covered in the Tarot cards section of this book, but it is possible using a purple crystal for this purpose

Love/Romance – Green crystals are normally the best for this type of reading

Work/Finances – Black or blue crystals tend to work best

Finally size – as I always say, size does not matter (pun intended) and I have found that ones that settle nicely in my palm of my hand are more comfortable and easier to read.

PREPARING YOUR CRYSTAL BALL – CLEANSING

As with all crystals, it is best to "charge" and cleanse your crystal ball when you first get this. This is not required after every reading but will be essential when you purchase them.

- Take your crystal ball in your hand and run this under cold water for about 1 to 2 minutes. As you are doing this ask your guides and Archangel Michael to bless the ball and to ask that the messages given are true and accurate.

- Place the ball on a window sill or where there is access to the Sun or Moonlight and leave it there for the duration. I tend to leave the ball in both (one day and one night). This will affect "charge" the ball ready for use.

Once you have completed the above then you are ready to start working with your crystal ball.

You should only need to do this once and you will find that people (especially children) want to play or touch your crystal ball. Personally, I don't mind and especially with children, it is fun as you can show them basic ways to start reading things in the crystal ball.

The question is does this not mean that there are now energies from other people on the ball? Yes and remember then you are reading (unlike tarot) your client will not be placing their energies on the ball. So cleanse before each reading I created a simple, quick and effective technique which helps will the ball cleansing before each reading.

- Take the ball into your dominant hand and place it onto the tarot cloth that you use for your readings

- Gently allow the ball to roll between your palm and/or fingers on the cloth

- As you do this just mentally ask the ball to be cleansed or keep saying cleanse for about 20 to 30 seconds.

WATCHING THE CLOUDS GO BY

As a child, I used to play games where I would look at the clouds and try to make out objects in the clouds (and I don't mean the rude ones either). It is a game that I still play to this day with my wife and is a great way to start getting to understand how to visualize and see shapes and objects in the crystal ball.

This process of seeing the object in clouds (and other areas too) has a scientific term which is Pareidolia and its definition is:

Definition of Pareidolia. : the tendency to perceive a specific, often meaningful image in a random or ambiguous visual pattern The scientific explanation for some people is Pareidolia, or the human ability to see shapes or make pictures out of randomness.

Unlike the science part or explanation, when you start working with the crystal ball, the objects or messages you see will have a specific meaning to the person for whom you are doing the reading for.

Playing the 'cloud game' even before you have purchased your crystal ball is a fantastic way to start and will also give you an idea right now if you will be able to see objects and patterns in the ball before you start.

Interesting enough this process is the same way that you read tea leaves and is a natural follow on from reading the crystal ball.

READING THE CRYSTAL BALL

I will be honest now and say this will be the hardest part but also the most fun part for you and the great thing is you can start straight away without having to understand what you are looking at or even for.

- With the ball in your hand (I tend to switch from my palm to holding in my fingers as I'm reading) look at the imperfections in the ball.

- Move the ball slowly around and back and forth, watching the imperfections and see how they change. You will notice that they will start to form symbols, numbers, and images that will appear. Sometimes you may have to move it backward and forward slowly to see them.

- Do not just look at the imperfections, but occasionally look "though" the ball as imperfections at the rear may interact with those closest to you

- Unfocused your eyes as this can sometimes assist with the reading

- As you become more confident with the ball you will start to see the image "moving". It's not uncommon for me to actually see loved ones or people in the crystal, talking and even passing the message.

- Take your time – to start with you need to just interact and work with the crystal and yourself to understand and connect with it.

Although this is the basics at this stage, this is a great way when it comes to picking your crystal.

When you are able to pick it up and the more you see within the imperfections, the better the crystal is for you!

With other types of balls that you can use i.e. such as birthstones for readings, you will not be able to 'see through the ball' as these tend to be more solid. Instead, you will look at the imperfections and patterns presented before you on the ball.

For me I will tend to stick to the Crystal – it is more fun, easier to use and can give you a lot more information.

HOW TO GAIN YOUR BASE READING

With each reading you do, you will need to start with a base reading with yourself first and this is simply to understand Yes and No answers in the crystal.

This will be your first time to start working with the crystal ball and will be the only time you will ask for a defined and constant image for the Yes and No answers.

- Taking the crystal in your hand ask a number of questions that you already know the answers too. These questions must have only a yes or no answers to them

- An example question might be "Is my name (insert your name)?" or is my favorite color Blue?

- For each answer to the yes or no, note the symbol you are drawn too. It should be the same symbol each time i.e. a yes might be a circle and a no might be a square.

This is to gain your base reading for Yes and No questions. You may find that you get a Y for Yes and an N for No – this is very common.

Once you are confident with your yes and no base reading then keep practicing it. Most of the questions people will ask (after their initial question) will be a yes or no answer and so will be the most important elements in your readings.

INTERPRETATION

When you are connected with your client, interpretation of the symbols really comes down to how you "feel" (instinct) or what information is being provided by your guides.

As with everything the more questions you ask, the better the reading. So, for example, you may see a letter A in the reading and feel that this is connected to a person with that letter. You could ask further questions – is this person male/female? Does my client already know them? Are there any potential issues around this person? Again use your base Yes and No symbols to help you at this stage.

And so on, so just picking up a symbol or letter, you can go deeper into the reading for the client, getting more information as much as possible.

With capital letters, I find that these tend to be the start of a name. This could be a person, a location such as a street name or anything that gives a defined persona meaning.

Whilst carrying out a reading for one client I actually saw in the crystal ball a person's name appears. The name Emma appeared and this had a huge significance for my client at that time as it was a connection with a loved one who had passed and someone she had been trying to connect with through other readers.

People's names or even partial names will often appear in the crystal ball and this is great confirmation. Place names will come through and this can help in searching for a person, animal or even an object.

The thing is not to try and over push these things as the more relaxed you are the easier it is for the symbols to come through.

WORKING WITH NUMBERS

These two can have meaning but at their simplest format can mean anything depicting a date or time factor i.e. the number 5 might for days, weeks, months even years.

A question might be "When will I expect to see a result in this matter?" and a number is then given to indicate a completion around this.

I had one client who asked when I expected her to get a response around issues she been having with her work. I advised that she would get a response very quickly but had the number 30 appear in the crystal – 30 seconds later she received a text message with the information she had been waiting on!

I honestly not sure who was more surprised at this – me or her.

Numbers can also mean the following but not restricted to – again use these guidelines nothing more:

1 – New start, being alone, birth, new beginnings

2 – Balance, harmony, reunion, meeting new people, choice, change

3 – Growth, life heartbreak, meeting old friends, communication

4 – Family, home, finances, bad luck, warning, feeling or being trapped or lost

5 – Instability, loss, split, division, disappointment

6 – Change, journey, travel, transition

7 – Mystery, uncertainty, change in the situation, new perspective

8 – Prosperity, moving on, gain, growth (8 is considered to be lucky)

9 – Fortune, good luck, completion

SYMBOLS AND OBJECTS

As with numbers and letters, symbols also play a big part in any reading and although the following (again) should be used purely as guidelines. I personally still prefer using my guides/instincts for each and suggest putting together a list of those objects you see more often as you do readings.

APPLE

An apple can represent health or the need to seek medical advice. It also has a bearing on study or new learning

ARROW

A direct indication of where someone needs to be looking in their life at that time (see left and right meanings in the next chapter). Pointing up may mean growth, down may mean getting back to basics

BAT

Tends to mean good news or messages from a loved one who has passed is trying to communicate

BELL

Action is required on an issue. It can also be used as a warning.

BIRD

Communication with some who is distant (physically or emotionally), and can also be an indication of travel but not a great distance.

BOAT

Travel of a distance is required or will be needed. Also, stability around a situation is needed

BOOK

Study or development (personal or work) is required or needs to be undertaken. If seen with a screen indicates an online study or training.

BROOM

Marriage or clearing out the old and bringing in the new

BUTTERFLY

Growth and transformation, new beginnings normally on a spiritual level

CANDLE

Guidance or start of a new path or journey

CAR

Also, it can mean travel but depends on the car. If you see the car changing can indicate what change a person is going through. Also can represent a physical car

CHAIR

Stability required time to be patient around a situation or the need to wait/slow down

COIN

Finances, wealth, property. Seeing a number of coins may indicate a financial gain, whilst seeing coins disappear my indicate an upcoming loss

CROSS

Faith, protection or even coming to a crossroads in the person life

CUP

Emotions, family, relationships

DEER

Strength (lion also gives this) – mentally or physically. Also alertness or the need to be on the lookout for a potential situation or problem

DOG

Loyalty, trust, and companionship

EYE

This can be around protection but also a change in the persons' spiritual journey i.e. the third eye

FISH

Representation of wisdom, knowledge, and understanding

GUN

Representation of focus, energy, and action needing to be taken quickly

HEART

Love and emotion – two hearts might be a union or commitment, a single heart may mean love from an admirer or learning love oneself. A broken heart may mean a split or an upset in a relationship

HORSE

Depends on the horse – a shire horse may mean hard work is required, whilst a racing horse may indicate a quick decision or an urgent matter needs to be resolved

HOUSE

Security, stability, and family. I have also found the house to mean a move or even pending work is required on a home.

KEY

Secrets need to be kept or being kept. Also a period of waiting for a new opportunity to present itself (doors being opened).

MOON

Fertility but also for new beginnings. Can also represent cycles or something that is not completed and needs to be revisited

PYRAMID

Stability, foundation but can also have a direct meaning for Egypt or Africa in general

RINGS

Can mean marriage or the bonding of two people or situations

SWORD

Conflicts, issues, concerns. Fighting battles or overcoming upcoming problems in a person's life

SNAKE

Long life and health but also can represent change or shedding of the old to bring in the new

TRIANGLE

In this, the number 3 is more appropriate. It can also point to teamwork or working within a team. The needing to bring in help or a third person for success

WAND

Dreams, desires, passions. Where a person needs to move forward with their desires or let go in order to move forward

WOLF

Protection, strength, unity

These really are just the start but will give you a basic guide to some symbols I have come across.

You can also (as indicated in the list but in case you missed it) use the base meanings of the minor arcana cards for some of the objects:

CUPS (SUIT OF CUPS)

Feelings & Emotions (Family, Relationships, Business relationships, Friends)

Element: Water (Emotions, Opinion, Instinct)

Represented as Hearts in the Playing card deck

Out of the four suits, the Cups seems to be the stumbling block for most people, as there is no real connection between cups and relationships (unlike the other suits below). So this will be the one that you generally have to remember what cups are.

WANDS OR STICKS (SUIT OF WANDS)

Imagination & Creativity (Dreams, Desires, Work, Projects)

Element: Fire (Ambition, Power, Intuition)

Represented as Clubs in the Playing card deck

The wands card is easy to remember by thinking of a magician waving his wand and making dreams and ideas come true.

COINS OR MONEY (SUIT OF PENTACLES)

Money & Potential (Wealth, Earnings, Funding, Loss, Gain)

Element: Earth (Practical, Grounded, Sensations)

Represented as Diamonds in the Playing card deck

Pentacles look like money, simple as that. When you see the pentacles use the idea of finances and funding as your base for this symbol.

SWORDS (SUIT OF SWORDS)

Life Challenges (Conflicts, Challenges, Troubles, Issues, Concerns)
Element: Air (Concepts, Thinking, Reasoning)
Represented as Spades in the Playing card deck

The swords again you use the idea of going to battle or fighting. This is a good base to use for this symbol.

Now you can see how tarot and crystal ball are starting to work very closely with each other. When I'm reading tarot I may often use the crystal ball in conjunction with some of the cards to further clarify the reading.

LEFT AND RIGHT MEANINGS

As with Tarot, the objects pointing or coming from the left and the right have the same definition. You will see objects coming from the left or the right-hand side of the ball as you look at it or maybe pointing in that direction.

An example of this is you may see gun pointing from the right to the left which may indicate action is required very soon in the future. Again ask the question, when it will be required (get a number) and in what is of the person's life (professional, personal, social and so on)

As a reminder from the tarot cards reading…

LEFT MEANING

Anything coming from the left will represents feminine or has to do with the past. The easy way to remember this is that your left arm is closest to your heart (love) for females.

RIGHT MEANING

Anything coming from the right will represent masculine or has to do with the future.

As a side note to this, if you ever decide to do tea leaf readings, then holding the cup with the handle pointing to your right-hand side. Any objects to the top/left of the handle are the past/female and any objects from the bottom/right of the handle are future/male

Divination comes in many ways but the basic principles are always the same.

The next few chapters have already been covered under the Tarot reading section of the book. Initially, I was going to just reference back to these rather than writing them again, however, there is some minor difference and also by repeating these, it reminds you of what we have already discussed.

Furthermore, it saves you having to flip back through the book to find these and for those that have skipped to the Crystal ball section then they have it to hand as well!

PREPARING FOR A READING

Preparation is so important for any reading. Sometimes it's not possible, especially if doing a group reading or someone asks you out of the blue to do one. I recall when I first started to do readings at fayres and I thought what on earth has I gotten into?

The thing is you can do as much or as little as you want in preparation, and the more you do the better the reading.

Two important things to remember about the following. You should use this as much as you can for both tarot and ball readings and also this can be used for distance readings as well. I suggest when you first start to use these as a guideline and as you develop and grow into the readings that you work with those sections that work best for you.

- Meditate the day before the reading. Connect with your client (you just need their first name only) and ask your Spirit Guide(s) to come forward. If you are not aware of your guides, then please use your intuition for the readings, but asking for them to come forward will also help you to develop a connection with them over a period of time.

- Make a note of any images, smells, intuition, even pains that you get. You do not need to write these down as your Spirit Guide(s) will bring these back to you during the reading IF they are relevant at that time.

- NO alcohol or caffeine at least 2 hours before the reading or during the reading and it is advisable to stick to water. This is not because if any dangers other than alcohol tend to loosen your tongue and that you may actually be the way to open during the reading.

- Have a comfortable place to sit, for you and your client. On the table have a lighted white candle (Spirit are drawn to white candles)

- A box of tissues handy nearby. You will need these and the number of times I have not put out tissues and asked clients if they want them to be told no, only to find they are in floods of tears at the end of the first card.

- Your tarot cloth for the cards to be placed upon during the reading.

- Glasses of water for you and your client.

WHEN YOUR CLIENT SITS FOR THE READING

Unless your client has had a reading before, then for many this will be a nerve-racking time. After all, they do not know what to expect and (in most cases) will already have pre-conceived ideas.

For this reason, it is important that you talk with your client first to understand what it is they are looking for from a reading. Is it a general reading or do they have specific questions that they would like to be answered?

In the case of the latter its best if the client does NOT give their questions to start with as this will dilute the reading. Instead, advise the client that any questions they have can be asked at the end of the reading.

I tend to start by going through the code of ethics of which there is an example that I use below. It's a bit like a doctor/patient confidentiality verbal agreement between you and your client. Remember, if they have never had a reading before, the chances are they will be nervous and this is a great opportunity to calm them down and to allow them to open up.

EXAMPLE CODE OF ETHICS

The following is the code of ethics I use with all my students and all my clients. You will be surprised how many readers do NOT have any form of code of ethics which shows lack of training and respect for their clients

- You can only give them what has been given to you by your Spirit Guide(s). If you are not meant to know something or it's not relevant at that time, it will not be given.

- What is said in the room is between you and them only. If the client wants to repeat what was said to friends afterward that's up to them

- If something is given which the client does not know or understand just ask them to accept it as it might mean something later on.

- If at any point the client wishes to stop the reading they can do so. Simply close down the reading and bring the session to a close.

- If they are not sure of anything, have a question or need clarification during the reading, remind them to just ask. The reading is for them and will (hopefully) be a great experience for them.

- If the client wants to record the reading or take notes, allow them. It adds to your credibility and also will help the client days later when they want to refer back to the reading.

- Tell them the more open they are and relaxed, the better the reading will be.

Unlike tarot, you will not be keeping your eyes closed during the reading as well, you won't be able to see or interpret the meanings of the symbols.

What you will find is that you will be so focused on the crystal ball and looking for the symbols that you will, in fact, won't be looking at your client during the session anyway.

HOW TO CONNECT WITH YOUR CLIENT

Once you are ready remember to connect with your client by creating an umbilical cord that does a figure 8 between you and your client (as described above).

Many readers do not even carry out this practice which then asks the question of how they are even working with their client.

You can also connect to any person regardless of their location. This is ideal if you are doing distance readings and you only need the person's first name. Some readers will ask for the date of birth as well but this really is not necessary.

You can also connect to people in a social environment as well in this manner but just be careful, as once you are connected you will start to see images and get a lot about the person the second you connect.

It is also worth noting that the hardest people to connect to are men (in general) and other light-workers. Just be careful who you connect with

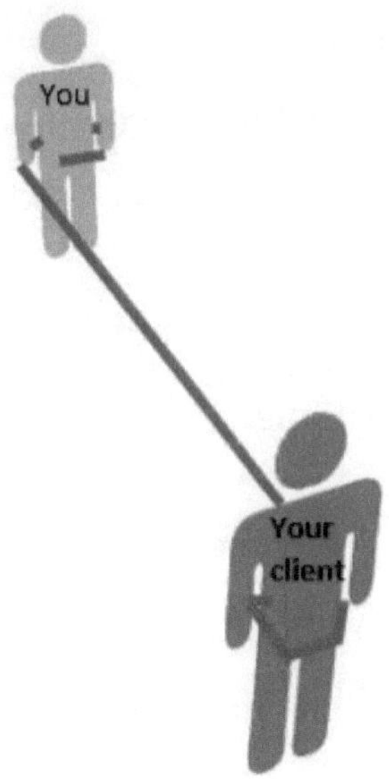

When you have completed the reading, remember to disconnect my visualizing a pair of scissors cutting the cord and then asking Archangel Michael to help heal and seal the ends.

Remember to open your chakras – for this, I will refer you back to the section of the chakras as outlined in the tarot reading section of this book!

CLOSING A READING

As with the Tarot, once you have completed your clients' reading please make sure they are ok. Ask them if they would like you to clarify any part of the reading back to them.

If all is completed then you need to carry out the final sections to close the reading.

- Unlink from your client. To do this imagine taking some scissors and cutting the umbilical cord that you created when you first linked up at the start of the reading.

- I tend to ask Archangel Michael to then bless and heal the cord ends.

- Close your chakras. Starting with your crown chakra imagine a lotus leaf closing around each one until only a pinprick of light is visible from each one. Do this until you get to your root chakra

- When your client has left carryout a grounding meditation/exercise.

If you can make or purchase a small cloth bag for your crystal ball just to keep it safe and protected. It is not necessary but is something that I personally do and as with the Tarot silks, it just protects the tools I use.

PAYMENT

You should never be concerned about being paid for your services. You are giving your time and energy for each reading and the Universe expects that you are paid.

Having a price list for each of your services is advisable and make sure your client knows your costs upfront.

There are two alternative ways I approach payments with clients:

1. Offset the payment with something in return such as a cake, a meal or even housework. If your client offers services such as Reiki, massage or hairdressing, see if they are willing to exchange services.

2. Donation option. If you do not want to have specific prices then just ask the person to donate an amount they feel comfortable with for the reading. I suggest you set a minimum amount though if you do use this option.

Finally, if you are really stuck, please visit my website www.markhoward.co.za and use the prices I charge as a guideline.

I have tried to keep my pricing very reasonable for my clients; without being too expensive.

You will get people trying to get free readings out of you and my response is don't! They will call you fake or anything to get you to change your mind and here is how I handled two different situations around this and to show you more how you should approach people like this.

FIRST SCENARIO

Lady asked me for free reading on one of the social media sites (tends to be where this occurs the most). She said that if I was really a Psychic (pampering to ego) that I would give an example reading and if I was good enough (ego again but her get out clause to not pay for a reading in the future), she would then pay for a reading and tell all her friends (which she won't).

MY RESPONSE

I asked the lady in question would she go to a restaurant and ask them if they can give her a free meal to try. If the meal was good enough that she would then go and pay for another meal later and then tell all her friends about the restaurant?

In short, people do not understand that your time and energy is being used when doing the readings and does not justify giving something for free. Another example of this is in my second scenario where again I was verbally attacked on a social media site for not giving another young lady a free reading.

SECOND SCENARIO

This woman started off by publically, verbally attacking me saying how disgusting it is that I have been given the gift (for free) to read cards and that I'm a disgrace to want to charge for my readings. Again she is attacking my ego and to add salt to the wound, shared this with all her friends and family.

MY RESPONSE

I started off by asking the women if she worked for a living or worked for someone. I then said does she not find it a disgrace that she has a gift or skill that she then gets paid for to do this work?

I then went on to explain that I, in fact, do NOT charge for any of my readings and that I do however charge for my time!

Consequently said post and comments were quickly removed by said person.

Do not fall into the trap of reading for free or for cheap. As my father used to say if you charge Tesco prices you get Tesco clients, charge Harrods prices you get Harrods clients.

I see many readers offering free readings on social media and they really get into a lot of issues. They get swamped with requests and then get knocked for being unable to deliver due to the high demand. And in the meantime this poor reader is doing literally 100's of readings, not getting paid and more importantly losing time and their daily life!

FINAL THOUGHTS

When you have completed the reading and your client has gone, you need to be aware of what's going on with yourself.

You will have used a lot of energy during the reading, and this can have a massive effect on you and this is regardless if you have done a tarot reading, crystal ball or any other form of divination.

With this in mind, the following pointers are always good and should be considered after each reading:

NOT BEING ABLE TO SLEEP AT NIGHT

Chances are you are still connected to your client OR you have not shut down your chakras.

Mentally cut the cord with your client and close your chakras. Finally, go through a grounding meditation.

FEELING TIRED, MENTALLY DRAINED OR EVEN SICK

This tends to be the following day and in the early days of you reading when you are reading for one or two clients in a day should not be an issue. If you start to do the tarot parties then this is when you will be most hit by this.

If you are able to take the following day off and rest. Drink plenty of fluids and relax. If possible go out and walk within Mother Nature to help you get your energy levels back.

THE MIND KEEPS DRIFTING OR YOU FEEL NOT YOURSELF.

Simply put you are not grounded and you need to go through a grounding meditation to clear your thoughts.
If possible wear something red (red socks for example) or walk around barefoot until you feel yourself. A cold shower also helps with this process

And so congratulations, if you follow all the principles I have set out in this book, you will find that you will be able to give accurate and credible readings for friends, family and even clients.

There is one person however, that you need to start reading for the moment you have completed this book and that person is you!

Reading for yourself is one of the hardest things to do and I can speak from my own personal experience that self-readings are difficult because you are second-guessing yourself the whole time.

Reading for yourself will allow you to develop a strong connection with your guides, help with your self-confidence and also help with your ego suppression too.

For this, I always ask my students to carry out the following homework for the first month to get used to working with your cards (you can even do this with your crystal ball as well).

DAILY EXERCISE

Every morning pull a single card for the day for yourself. Look at it for no more than 30 seconds and take on board any information you have been given for the day. Place the card back and enjoy your day.

WEEKLY EXERCISE

Once a week (you decide which day), carryout a three-card reading for yourself for the coming week. Again should take no more than ten minutes to complete and make notes of your reading to refer back to later.

MONTHLY EXERCISE

At the end of the month do a five-card reading for the coming month for yourself. Again this should take no more than twenty minutes and remember to make notes throughout the reading.

I suggest doing this for one month only but I have students that have done two even three months of this and found not only have they become confident readers, but they have also seen a huge change in their lives as well.

THE CHAKRA GUIDE

If you are not sure about your Chakras, location and colouring, then please use the following image as a guide and refer back to the chakra section in this book.

I placed the image here at the back of the book as an easy and quick location for you find it.

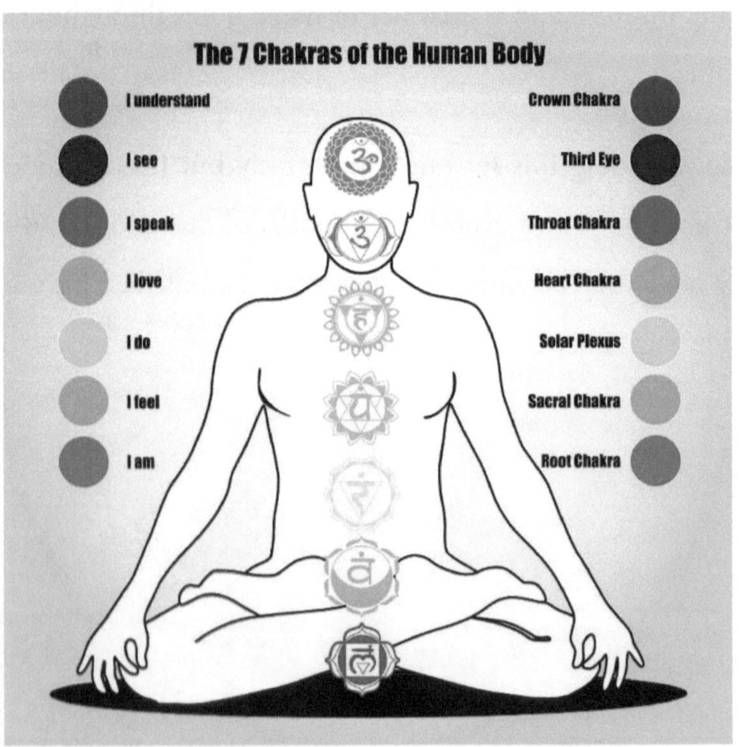

www.ingramcontent.com/pod-product-compliance
Lightning Source LLC
Chambersburg PA
CBHW031335060726
47590CB00007B/2480